I0821018

A Human Approach to World Peace

A Human Approach to World Peace

HIS HOLINESS TENZIN GYATSO

DALAI LAMA XIV

Foreword by Richard Gere

Wisdom Publications
132 Perry Street
New York, NY 10014 USA
wisdom.org

© 2025 Gaden Phodrang Foundation of the Dalai Lama
All rights reserved.

No part of this book may be reproduced in any form or by any means, electronic or mechanical, including photography, recording, or by any information storage and retrieval system or technologies now known or later developed, without permission in writing from the publisher.

LCCN 2025934434
ISBN 979-8-89070-043-8 ebook ISBN 979-8-89070-033-9

30 29 28 27 26 5 4 3 2 1

Cover and interior design by Gopa & Ted 2, Inc.
The image of Palden Lhamo on page 62 is from the 1895 book *Tibetan Buddhism* by L. Austine Waddell.

Printed on acid-free paper that meets the guidelines for permanence and durability of the Production Guidelines for Book Longevity of the Council on Library Resources.

Printed in Canada.

Contents

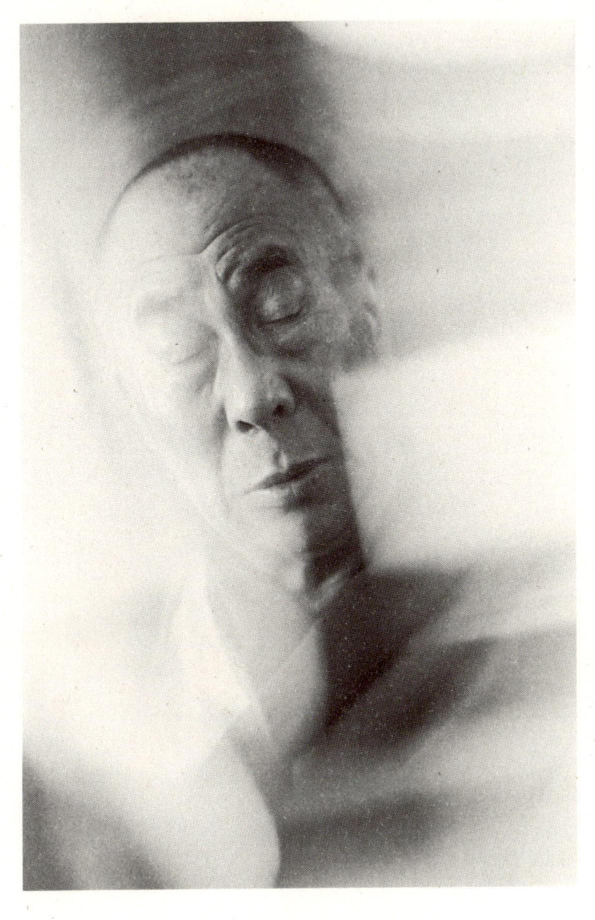

Publisher's Acknowledgment

THE PUBLISHER gratefully acknowledges the generous help of the International Campaign for Tibet in sponsoring the production of this book in honor of His Holiness the Dalai Lama's ninetieth birthday.

Foreword

THERE ARE some beings who just shine with more light, who have worked on themselves, over many lifetimes, with more effort and courage than the rest of us, who are as vast as the infinite universes. His Holiness the Dalai Lama is such a one, as rare as a star in the midday sky.

As we enter this, His Holiness's ninetieth year, on this small, beautiful planet that we all call home, it is an enormous pleasure to honor his extraordinary life of service with this jewel-like book, which was first published forty years ago.

In the mid-1980s, I had just returned from a devastating trip through a Central America that was burning in violence. Honduras, El Salvador, Nicaragua. Farabundo Martí National Liberation Front guerrillas, refugee camps, secret US bases, embassies, Contras, Sandinistas, doctors, priests, nuns, aid workers, farmers, poets, death squads. Cruelty, madness, horror, hope . . . My brothers and sisters of different languages and different cultures were suffering enormously. They were all looking for happiness and trying to escape pain and suffering. Just like you and me, in our own ways.

When I returned home to New York, dazed and lost, my Tibetan friends gave to me this precious little book written by His Holiness, *A Human Approach To World Peace*. I read it and reread it, I underlined it, I put it on my altar. It challenged me. It provoked me. It helped me make sense of the senseless, of the cruelty and violence. How can we end suffering in ourselves and in our world? For everyone? Yes, everyone.

Where does the healing begin?

Forty years later I still find this small book to be enormously powerful and relevant. We gratefully honor these most profound ninety years of the Dalai Lama's precious life and teachings on wisdom, love, and responsibility. I know that His Holiness would only ask of us that we generate in our deepest hearts and minds the purest commitment to be more wise, more loving, and more kind, to allow our pure light to shine more brightly in ourselves, our families, and our world, beyond all illusory and artificial borders, beyond self-interest. Beyond self-cherishing.

As His Holiness assures us, we can heal ourselves and our world. The healing has begun if we want it.

Richard Gere, chairman,
International Campaign for Tibet

Introduction

WHEN WE RISE in the morning and listen to the radio or read the newspaper, we are confronted with the same sad news: violence, crime, wars, and disasters. I cannot recall a single day without a report of something terrible happening somewhere. Even in these modern times it is clear that one's precious life is not safe. No former generation has had to experience so much bad news as we face today; this constant awareness of fear and tension should make any sensitive and compassionate person question seriously the progress of our modern world.

It is ironic that the more serious problems emanate from the more industrially advanced societies. Science and technology have worked wonders in many fields, but the basic human problems remain. There is unprecedented literacy, yet this universal education does not seem to have fostered

goodness but only mental restlessness and discontent instead. There is no doubt about the increase in our material progress and technology, but somehow this is not sufficient, as we have not yet succeeded in bringing about peace and happiness or in overcoming suffering.

We can only conclude that there must be something seriously wrong with our progress and development, and if we do not check it in time, there could be disastrous consequences for the future of humanity. I am not at all against science and technology—they have contributed immensely to the overall experience of humankind: to our material comfort and well-being, and our greater understanding of the world we live in. But if we give too much emphasis to science and technology, we are in danger of losing touch with those aspects of human knowledge and understanding that inspire us toward honesty and altruism.

Science and technology, though capable of creating immeasurable material comfort, cannot replace the age-old spiritual and humanitarian values that have largely shaped world civilization, in all its national forms, as we know it today. No one can deny the unprecedented material benefit of science and technology, but our basic human problems remain; we are still faced with the same, if not more, suffering, fear, and tension. Thus, it is only logical to try to strike a balance between material developments on the one hand and the development of spiritual, human values on the other. In order to bring about this great adjustment, we need to revive our humanitarian values.

I am sure that many people share my concern about the present worldwide moral crisis and will join in my appeal to all humanitarians and religious practitioners who also share this concern to help make our societies more compassionate, just, and equitable. I do not speak as a Buddhist or even as a Tibetan. Nor do I speak as an expert on international politics (though I unavoidably comment on these matters). Rather, I speak simply as a human being, as an upholder of the humanitarian values that are the bedrock not only of Mahayana Buddhism but of all the great world religions. From this perspective I share with you my personal outlook:

1. Universal humanitarianism is essential to solve global problems.
2. Compassion is the pillar of world peace.
3. All world religions are already for world peace in this way, as are all humanitarians of whatever ideology.
4. Each individual has a universal responsibility to shape institutions to serve human needs.

Solving Human Problems through Transforming Human Attitudes

OF THE many problems we face today, some are natural calamities and must be accepted and faced with equanimity. Others, however, are of our own making, created by misunderstanding, and can be corrected. One such type arises from the conflict of ideologies, political or religious, when people fight each other for petty ends, losing sight of the basic humanity that binds us all together as a single human family. We must remember that the different religions, ideologies, and political systems of the world are meant for human beings to achieve happiness. We must not lose sight of this fundamental goal, and at no time should we place means above ends; the supremacy of humanity over matter and ideology must always be maintained.

By far the greatest single danger facing humankind—in fact, all living beings on our planet—is the threat of nuclear destruction. I need not elaborate on this danger, but I would like to appeal to all the leaders of the nuclear powers who literally hold the future of the world in their hands, to the scientists and technicians who continue to create these awesome weapons of destruction, and to all the people at large who are in a position to influence their leaders: I appeal to them to exercise their sanity and begin to work at dismantling and destroying all nuclear weapons. We know that in the event of a nuclear war there will be no victors because there will be no survivors! Is it not frightening just to contemplate such inhuman and heartless destruction? And is it not logical that we should remove the cause for our own destruction when we know the cause and have both the time and the means to do so? Often we cannot overcome our problems because we either do not know the cause or, if we understand it, do not have the means to remove it. This is not the case with the nuclear threat.

Whether they belong to more evolved species like humans or to simpler ones such as animals, all beings primarily seek peace, comfort, and security.

Life is as dear to the mute animal as it is to any human being; even the simplest insect strives for protection from dangers that threaten its life. Just as each one of us wants to live and does not wish to die, so it is with all other creatures in the universe, though their power to effect this is a different matter.

Broadly speaking there are two types of happiness and suffering—mental and physical—and of the two, I believe that *mental* suffering and happiness are the more acute. Hence, I stress the training of the mind to endure suffering and attain a more lasting state of happiness. However, I also have a more general and concrete idea of happiness: a combination of inner peace, economic development, and above all, world peace. To achieve such goals, I feel it is necessary to develop a sense of *universal responsibility*, a deep concern for all, irrespective of creed, color, sex, or nationality.

The premise behind this idea of universal responsibility is the simple fact that, in general terms, all others' desires are the same as mine. Every being wants happiness and does not want suffering. If we, as intelligent human beings, do not accept this fact, there will be more and more suffering on this planet. If we adopt a self-centered approach to life and constantly try to use others for our own self-interest, we may gain temporary benefits, but in the long run we will not succeed in achieving even personal happiness, and world peace will be completely out of the question.

In their quest for happiness, humans have used different methods, which all too often have been cruel and repellent. Behaving in ways utterly unbecoming to their status as humans, they inflict suffering upon fellow humans and other living beings for their own selfish gains. In the end, such short-sighted actions bring suffering to oneself as well as to others. To be born a human being is a rare event in itself, and it is wise to use this opportunity as effectively and skillfully as possible. We must have the proper perspective, that of the universal life process, so that the happiness or glory of one person or group is not sought at the expense of others.

All this calls for a new approach to global problems. The world is becoming smaller and smaller—and more and more interdependent—as a result of rapid technological advances and international trade as well as increasing transnational relations. We now depend very much on each other. In ancient times problems were mostly family sized, and they were naturally tackled at the family level, but the situation has changed. Today we are so interdependent, so closely interconnected with each other, that without a sense of universal responsibility, a feeling of universal brotherhood and sisterhood, and an understanding and belief that we really are part of one big *human* family, we cannot hope to overcome the dangers to our very existence—let alone bring about peace and happiness.

One nation's problems can no longer be satisfactorily solved by itself alone; too much depends on the interest, attitude, and cooperation of other nations. A universal humanitarian approach to world problems seems the only sound basis for world peace. What does this mean? We begin from the recognition, mentioned previously, that all beings cherish happiness and do not want suffering. It then becomes both morally wrong and pragmatically unwise to pursue only one's own happiness oblivious to the feelings and aspirations of all others who surround us as members of the same human family. The wiser course is to think of others also when pursuing our own happiness. This will lead to what I call "wise self-interest," which hopefully will transform itself into "compromised self-interest," or better still, "mutual interest."

Although the increasing interdependence among nations might be expected to generate more sympathetic cooperation, it is difficult to achieve a spirit of genuine cooperation as long as people remain indifferent to the feelings and happiness of others. When people are motivated mostly by greed and jealousy, it is not possible for them to live in harmony. A spiritual approach may not solve all the political problems that have been caused by the existing self-centered approach, but in the long run it will overcome the very basis of the problems that we face today.

On the other hand, if humankind continues to approach its problems considering only temporary expediency, future generations will have to face tremendous difficulties. The global population is increasing, and our resources are being rapidly depleted. Look at the trees, for example. No one knows exactly what adverse effects massive deforestation will have on the climate, the soil, and global ecology as a whole. We are facing problems because people are concentrating only on their short-term, selfish interests, not thinking of the entire human family. They are not thinking of the earth and the long-term effects on universal life as a whole. If we of the present generation do not think about these now, future generations may not be able to cope with them.

Compassion as the Pillar of World Peace

According to Buddhist psychology, most of our troubles are due to our passionate desire for and attachment to things that we misapprehend as enduring entities. The pursuit of the objects of our desire and attachment involves the use of aggression and competitiveness as supposedly efficacious instruments. These mental processes easily translate into actions, breeding belligerence as an obvious effect. Such processes have been going on in the human mind since time immemorial, but their execution has become more effective under modern conditions. What can we do to control and regulate these "poisons"—delusion, greed, and aggression? For it is these poisons that are behind almost every trouble in the world.

As one brought up in the Mahayana Buddhist tradition, I feel that love and compassion are the moral fabric of world peace. Let me first define what I mean by compassion. When you have pity or compassion for a very poor person, you are showing sympathy because he or she is poor; your compassion is based on altruistic considerations. On the other hand, love toward your wife, your husband, your children, or a close friend is usually based on attachment. When your attachment changes, your kindness also changes; it may disappear. This is not true love. Real love is not based on attachment but on altruism. In this case your compassion will remain as a humane response to suffering as long as beings continue to suffer.

This type of compassion is what we must strive to cultivate in ourselves, and we must develop it from a limited amount to the limitless. Undiscriminating, spontaneous, and unlimited compassion for all sentient beings is obviously not the usual love that one has for friends or family, which is alloyed with ignorance, desire, and attachment. The kind of love we should advocate is this wider love that you can have even for someone who has done harm to you: your enemy.

The rationale for compassion is that every one of us wants to avoid suffering and gain happiness.

This, in turn, is based on the valid feeling of "I," which determines the universal desire for happiness. Indeed, all beings are born with similar desires and should have an equal right to fulfill them. If I compare myself with others, who are countless, I feel that others are *more* important, because I am just one person whereas others are many. Further, the Tibetan Buddhist tradition teaches us to view all sentient beings as our dear mothers and to show our gratitude by loving them all. For, according to Buddhist theory, we are born and reborn countless numbers of times, and it is conceivable that each being has been our parent at one time or another. In this way all beings in the universe share a family relationship.

Whether one believes in religion or not, there is no one who does not appreciate love and compassion. Right from the moment of our birth, we are under the care and kindness of our parents; later in life, when facing the sufferings of disease and old age, we are again dependent on the kindness of others. If at the beginning and end of our lives we depend upon others' kindness, why then in the middle should we not act kindly toward others?

The development of a kind heart (a feeling of closeness for all human beings) does not involve the religiosity we normally associate with conventional religious practice. It is not only for people who believe in religion but is for everyone, regardless of race, religion, or political affiliation. It is for anyone who considers himself or herself, above all, a member of the human family and who sees things from this larger and longer perspective. This is a powerful feeling that we should develop and apply; instead, we often neglect it, particularly in our prime years, when we experience a false sense of security.

When we take into account a longer perspective, the fact that all wish to gain happiness and avoid suffering, and keep in mind our relative unimportance in relation to countless others, we can conclude that it is worthwhile to share our possessions with others. When you train in this sort of outlook, a true sense of compassion—a true sense of love and respect for others—becomes possible. Individual happiness ceases to be a conscious self-seeking effort; it becomes an automatic and far superior by-product of the whole process of loving and serving others.

Another result of spiritual development, most useful in day-to-day life, is a calmness and presence of mind. Our lives are in constant flux, bringing many difficulties. When faced with a calm and clear mind, problems can be successfully resolved. When, instead, we lose control over our minds through hatred, selfishness, jealousy, and anger, we lose our sense of judgement. Our minds are blinded and at those wild moments anything can happen, including war. Thus, the practice of compassion and wisdom is useful to all, especially to those responsible for running national affairs, in whose hands lie the power and opportunity to create the structure of world peace.

World Religions for World Peace

THE PRINCIPLES discussed so far are in accordance with the ethical teachings of all world religions. I maintain that every major religion of the world—Buddhism, Christianity, Confucianism, Hinduism, Islam, Jainism, Judaism, Sikhism, Taoism, Zoroastrianism—has similar ideals of love, the same goal of benefiting humanity through spiritual practice, and the same effect of making their followers into better human beings. All religions teach moral precepts for perfecting the functions of mind, body, and speech. All teach us not to lie or steal or take others' lives, and so on. The common goal of all moral precepts laid down by the great teachers of humanity is unselfishness. The great teachers wanted to lead their followers away from the paths of negative deeds caused by ignorance and to introduce them to paths of goodness.

All religions agree upon the necessity to control

the undisciplined mind that harbors selfishness and other roots of trouble, and each teaches a path leading to a spiritual state that is peaceful, disciplined, ethical, and wise. It is in this sense that I believe all religions have essentially the same message. Differences of dogma may be ascribed to differences of time and circumstance as well as cultural influences; indeed, there is no end to scholastic argument when we consider the purely metaphysical side of religion. However, it is much more beneficial to try to implement in daily life the shared precepts for goodness taught by all religions, rather than to argue about minor differences in approach.

There are many different religions to bring comfort and happiness to humanity in much the same way as there are particular treatments for different diseases, for all religions endeavor in their own way to help living beings avoid misery and gain happiness. And, although we can find causes for preferring certain interpretations of religious truths, there is much greater cause for unity, stemming from the human heart. Each religion works in its own way to lessen human suffering and contribute to world civilization. Conversion is not the point.

For instance, I do not think of converting others to Buddhism or merely furthering the Buddhist cause. Rather, I try to think of how I as a Buddhist humanitarian can contribute to human happiness.

While pointing out the fundamental similarities between world religions, I do not advocate one particular religion at the expense of all others, nor do I seek a new "world religion." All the different religions of the world are needed to enrich human experience and world civilization. Our human minds, being of different caliber and disposition, need different approaches to peace and happiness. It is just like food. Certain people find Christianity more appealing; others prefer Buddhism because there is no creator in it and everything depends upon your own actions. We can make similar arguments for other religions as well. Thus, the point is clear: humanity needs all the world's religions to suit the ways of life, diverse spiritual needs, and inherited national traditions of individual human beings.

It is from this perspective that I welcome efforts being made in various parts of the world for better understanding among religions. The need for this

is particularly urgent now. If all religions make the betterment of humanity their main concern, then they can easily work together in harmony for world peace. Interfaith understanding will bring about the unity necessary for all religions to work together. However, although this is indeed an important step, we must remember that there are no quick or easy solutions. We cannot hide the doctrinal differences that exist among various faiths, nor can we hope to replace the existing religions with a new universal belief. Each religion has its own distinctive contributions to make, and each in its own way is suitable to a particular group of people as they understand life. The world needs them all.

There are two primary tasks facing religious practitioners who are concerned with world peace. First, we must promote better interfaith understanding so as to create a workable degree of unity among all religions. This may be achieved in part by respecting each other's beliefs and by emphasizing our common concern for human well-being. Second, we must bring about a viable consensus on basic spiritual values that touch every human heart and enhance general human happiness. This means we must emphasize the common denominator of all world religions—humanitarian ideals. These two steps will enable us to act both individually and together to create the necessary spiritual conditions for world peace.

We practitioners of different faiths can work together for world peace when we view different religions as essentially instruments to develop a good heart—love and respect for others, a true sense of community. The most important thing is to look at the purpose of religion and not at the details of theology or metaphysics, which can lead to mere intellectualism. I believe that all the major religions of the world can contribute to world peace and work together for the benefit of humanity if we put aside subtle metaphysical differences, which are really the internal business of each religion.

Despite the progressive secularization brought about by worldwide modernization and despite systematic attempts in some parts of the world to destroy spiritual values, the vast majority of humanity continues to believe in one religion or another. The undying faith in religion, evident even under irreligious political systems, clearly demonstrates the potency of religion as such. This spiritual energy and power can be purposefully used to bring about the spiritual conditions necessary for world peace. Religious leaders and humanitarians all over the world have a special role to play in this respect.

Whether we will be able to achieve world peace or not, we have no choice but to work toward that goal. If our minds are dominated by anger, we will lose the best part of human intelligence—wisdom, the ability to decide between right and wrong. Anger is one of the most serious problems facing the world today.

Individual Power to Shape Institutions

ANGER PLAYS no small role in current conflicts such as those in the Middle East, Southeast Asia, the North-South problem, and so forth. These conflicts arise from a failure to understand one another's humanness. The answer is not the development and use of greater military force, nor is it an arms race. Nor is it purely political or purely technological. Basically it is spiritual, in the sense that what is required is a sensitive understanding of our common human situation. Hatred and fighting cannot bring happiness to anyone, even to the winners of battles. Violence always produces misery and thus is essentially counterproductive. It is, therefore, time for world leaders to learn to transcend the differences of race, culture, and ideology and to regard one another through eyes that see the common human situation. To do so would benefit individuals, communities, nations, and the world at large.

The greater part of present world tension seems to stem from the "Eastern bloc" versus "Western bloc" conflict that has been going on since World War II. These two blocs tend to describe and view each other in a totally unfavorable light. This continuing, unreasonable struggle is due to a lack of mutual affection and respect for each other as fellow human beings. Those of the Eastern bloc should reduce their hatred toward the Western bloc, because the Western bloc is also made up of human beings—men, women, and children. Similarly those of the Western bloc should reduce their hatred toward the Eastern bloc, because the Eastern bloc is also human beings. In such a reduction of mutual hatred, the leaders of both blocs have a powerful role to play. But first and foremost, leaders must realize their own and others' humanness. Without this basic realization, very little effective reduction of organized hatred can be achieved.

If, for example, the leader of the United States of America and the leader of the Union of Soviet Socialist Republics suddenly met each other in the middle of a desolate island, I am sure they would respond to each other spontaneously as fellow human beings. But a wall of mutual suspicion and misunderstanding separates them the moment they are identified as the "President of the USA" and the "Secretary-General of the USSR." More human contact in the form of informal extended meetings, without any agenda, would improve their mutual understanding; they would learn to relate to each other as human beings and could then try to tackle international problems based on this understanding. No two parties, especially those with a history of antagonism, can negotiate fruitfully in an atmosphere of mutual suspicion and hatred.

I suggest that world leaders meet about once a year in a beautiful place without any business, just to get to know each other as human beings. Then, later, they could meet to discuss mutual and global problems. I am sure many others share my wish that world leaders meet at the conference table in such an atmosphere of mutual respect and understanding of each other's humanness.

To improve person-to-person contact in the world at large, I would like to see greater encouragement of international tourism. Also, mass media, particularly in democratic societies, can make a considerable contribution to world peace by giving greater coverage to human interest items that reflect the ultimate oneness of humanity. With the rise of a few big powers in the international arena, the humanitarian role of international organizations is being bypassed and neglected. I hope that this will be corrected and that all international organizations, especially the United Nations, will be more active and effective in ensuring maximum benefit to humanity and promoting international understanding. It will indeed be tragic if the few powerful members continue to misuse world bodies like the UN for their one-sided interests. The UN must become the instrument of world peace. This world body must be respected by all, for the UN is the only source of hope for small, oppressed nations and hence for the planet as a whole.

As all nations are economically dependent upon one another more than ever before, human understanding must go beyond national boundaries and embrace the international community at large. Indeed, unless we can create an atmosphere of genuine cooperation, gained not by threatened or actual use of force but by heartfelt understanding, world problems will only increase. If people in poorer countries are denied the happiness they desire and deserve, they will naturally be dissatisfied and pose problems for the rich. If unwanted social, political, and cultural forms continue to be imposed upon unwilling people, the attainment of world peace is doubtful. However, if we satisfy people at a heart-to-heart level, peace will surely come.

Within each nation, the individual ought to be given the right to happiness, and among nations, there must be equal concern for the welfare of even the smallest nations. I am not suggesting that one system is better than another and all should adopt it. On the contrary, a variety of political systems and ideologies is desirable and accords with the variety of dispositions within the human community. This variety enhances the ceaseless human quest for happiness. Thus each community should be free to evolve its own political and socioeconomic system, based on the principle of self-determination.

The achievement of justice, harmony, and peace depends on many factors. We should think about them in terms of human benefit in the long run rather than the short term. I realize the enormity of the task before us, but I see no other alternative than the one I am proposing—which is based on our common humanity. Nations have no choice but to be concerned about the welfare of others, not so much because of their belief in humanity, but because it is in the mutual and long-term interest of all concerned. An appreciation of this new reality is indicated by the emergence of regional or continental economic organizations such as the European Economic Community, the Association of Southeast Asian Nations, and so forth. I hope more such transnational organizations will be formed, particularly in regions where economic development and regional stability seem in short supply.

Under present conditions, there is definitely a growing need for human understanding and a sense of universal responsibility. In order to achieve such ideas, we must generate a good and kind heart, for without this, we can achieve neither universal happiness nor lasting world peace. We cannot create peace on paper. While we advocate universal responsibility and universal brotherhood and sisterhood, the facts are that humanity is organized in separate entities in the form of national societies. Thus, in a realistic sense, I feel it is these societies that must act as the building blocks for world peace.

Attempts have been made in the past to create societies more just and equal. Institutions have been established with noble charters to combat antisocial forces. Unfortunately, such ideas have been cheated by selfishness. More than ever before, we witness today how ethics and noble principles are obscured by the shadow of self-interest, particularly in the political sphere. There is a school of thought that warns us to refrain from politics altogether, as politics has become synonymous with amorality. Politics devoid of ethics does not further human welfare, and life without morality reduces humans to the level of beasts. However, politics is not axiomatically "dirty." Rather, the instruments of our political culture have distorted the high ideals and noble concepts meant to further human welfare. Naturally, spiritual people express their concern about religious leaders "messing" with politics, since they fear the contamination of religion by dirty politics.

I question the popular assumption that religion and ethics have no place in politics and that religious persons should seclude themselves as hermits. Such a view of religion is too one-sided; it lacks a proper perspective on the individual's relation to society and the role of religion in our lives. Ethics is as crucial to a politician as it is to a religious practitioner. Dangerous consequences will follow when politicians and rulers forget moral principles. Whether we believe in God or karma, ethics is the foundation of every religion.

Such human qualities as morality, compassion, decency, wisdom, and so forth have been the foundations of all civilizations. These qualities must be cultivated and sustained through systematic moral education in a conducive social environment so that a more humane world may emerge. The qualities required to create such a world must be inculcated right from the beginning, from childhood. We cannot wait for the next generation to make this change; the present generation must attempt a renewal of basic human values. If there is any hope, it is in the future generations, but not unless we institute major change on a worldwide scale in our present educational system. We need a revolution in our commitment to and practice of universal humanitarian values.

It is not enough to make noisy calls to halt moral degeneration; we must do something about it. Since present-day governments do not shoulder such "religious" responsibilities, humanitarian and religious leaders must strengthen the existing civic, social, cultural, educational, and religious organizations to revive human and spiritual values. Where necessary, we must create new organizations to achieve these goals. Only in so doing can we hope to create a more stable basis for world peace.

Living in society, we should share the sufferings of our fellow citizens and practice compassion and tolerance not only toward our loved ones but also toward our enemies. This is the test of our moral strength. We must set an example by our own practice, for we cannot hope to convince others of the value of religion by mere words. We must live up to the same high standards of integrity and sacrifice that we ask of others. The ultimate purpose of all religions is to serve and benefit humanity. This is why it is so important that religion always be used to effect the happiness and peace of all beings and not merely to convert others.

Still, in religion there are no national boundaries. A religion can and should be used by any people or person who finds it beneficial. What is important for each seeker is to choose a religion that is most suitable to himself or herself. But the embracing of a particular religion does not mean the rejection of another religion or one's own community. In fact, it is important that those who embrace a religion should not cut themselves off from their own society; they should continue to live within their own community and in harmony with its members. By escaping from your own community, you cannot benefit others, whereas benefiting others is actually the basic aim of religion.

In this regard there are two things important to keep in mind: self-examination and self-correction. We should constantly check our attitude toward others, examining ourselves carefully, and we should correct ourselves immediately when we find we are in the wrong.

Finally, a few words about material progress. I have heard a great deal of complaint against material progress from Westerners, and yet, paradoxically, it has been the very pride of the Western world. I see nothing wrong with material progress per se, provided *people* are always given precedence. It is my firm belief that in order to solve human problems in all their dimensions, we must combine and harmonize economic development with spiritual growth.

However, we must know its limitations. Although materialistic knowledge in the form of science and technology has contributed enormously to human welfare, it is not capable of creating lasting happiness. In America, for example, where technological development is perhaps more advanced than in any other country, there is still a great deal of mental suffering. This is because materialistic knowledge can only provide a type of happiness that is *dependent* upon physical conditions. It cannot provide happiness that springs from inner development *independent of external factors.*

For renewal of human values and attainment of lasting happiness, we need to look to the common humanitarian heritage of all nations the world over. May this essay serve as an urgent reminder lest we forget the human values that unite us all as a single family on this planet.

I have written the above lines
To tell my constant feeling.
Whenever I meet even a "foreigner,"
I have always the same feeling:
"I am meeting another member of the
human family."
This attitude has deepened
My affection and respect for all beings.
May this natural wish be
My small contribution to world peace.
I pray for a more friendly,
More caring, and more understanding
Human family on this planet.
To all who dislike suffering,
Who cherish lasting happiness—
This is my heartfelt appeal.

Addendum: Forty Years Later

When I initially expressed my thoughts in the small booklet *A Human Approach to World Peace*, it was the 1980s, and I was in my fifties. Since then, several decades have passed. We are now in the third decade of the twenty-first century, and I am entering my nineties. Even though the world has seen much change, both positive and negative, since the appearance of that booklet, I am convinced that the fundamental issues I raised continue to be valid. Indeed, the need to strive for peace has lately become even more critical due to rapid developments in science and technology that are making it easier for those who wish to make trouble to have their way.

When, in the past, men fought with swords or spears, they could only do limited damage. Today, the use of weapons of immense destructive potential has become commonplace. They were developed by scientists and technologists with the finest brains and the highest educations, which, although they may not have intended it, had become focused on refining the means to kill.

The twentieth century was a century of war and bloodshed. In my essay, I mentioned that there was a worldwide lack of human values, and that if we did not address this in time, the consequences for the future of humanity could be disastrous. Unfortunately, that threat continues to haunt us today.

The responsibility of ensuring that this new, twenty-first century becomes an era of dialogue and diplomacy, rather than one of war and bloodshed, belongs to us all. There will always be disputes and disagreements among human beings—but they can and should be resolved through dialogue and discussion. In my original essay, I addressed the issue of global peace via four points: universal humanitarianism is essential to solve global problems; compassion is the pillar of world peace; all world religions are already for world peace in this way, as are all humanitarians of whatever ideology; and each individual has a universal responsibility to shape institutions to serve human needs. As a member of the human family, I have tried to contribute to the promotion of peace by upholding these four commitments; I outline some of my efforts below.

Firstly, I have drawn attention to something we humans all have in common: we all want to be happy and none of us wants to suffer. I have advocated the cultivation of warm-heartedness and such human values as compassion, forgiveness, tolerance, contentment, and self-discipline. I refer to these principles as secular or universal values because they transcend specific religious boundaries. These values enable us to remember the oneness of humanity and think of each other first and foremost as fellow human beings. I have expanded on this in my books *Ethics for the New Millennium* and *Beyond Religion: Ethics for a Whole World*, which emphasize a moral system based on such universal humanitarian principles.

Secondly, although I am a Buddhist monk and find Buddhism to be most satisfying for me, I respect all religious traditions. For this reason, I have encouraged harmony, based on understanding, among the world's religions. Despite philosophical differences between them, all the major world religions have the potential to create good human beings. It is therefore important for all of them to respect one another and recognize the value of their particular traditions. I articulated my thoughts about this in the book *Toward a True Kinship of Faiths*, in which I suggested we should appreciate differences of approach between religious traditions, because they suit people's different dispositions.

Thirdly, I am a Tibetan and the "Dalai Lama," and the Tibetan people place their hopes and trust in me. What has been important to us is our belief that Tibetan Buddhist culture—a culture of peace, a culture of compassion, and a culture of nonviolence—is something worth preserving for the benefit of the world. Therefore, I have been working to preserve Tibetan language and culture, the heritage Tibetans received from the masters of India's Nalanda tradition, while also speaking up for the protection of Tibet's natural environment. Obviously, a mutually acceptable, peaceful resolution of the Tibetan issue will enable us Tibetans to achieve these goals while preserving our identity.

Lastly, I am convinced that the ancient Indian

understanding of the workings of the mind and emotions, as well as techniques of mental training such as meditation, is of great relevance today. I also believe India's ancient knowledge, when viewed from a secular, universal perspective, can be combined with modern education. I learned from the Nalanda tradition how to preserve my own peace of mind, and I am convinced that through education we can make such knowledge more widely available to the benefit of all humanity. Although ancient India's understanding of the workings of the mind and emotions grew out of its religious traditions, what we need today is an education of the mind and heart in a format that is secular and universal.

Once children enter into the modern education system, there's not much talk about human values. They become oriented toward material goals while their positive inner qualities lie dormant. Education should help us use our intelligence to good effect, which means we must be realistic, guided by reason and common sense.

I hope and wish that, one day, formal education will include what I call education of the heart. Just as we teach children to pay attention to their physical health through good hygiene, we should also teach them how to pay attention to their mental well-being through good emotional hygiene by tackling destructive emotions like anger and fear. I look forward to a day when children and students are more aware of their feelings and emotions and feel a greater sense of responsibility for themselves and the wider world.

I have therefore engaged in numerous dialogues with educationists in various parts of the world, including Asia, Europe, and North America, exploring how this vision of an education of the heart could be brought into reality. Today, I am happy to know that the teaching of social and emotional skills has become quite customary in many schools. I understand efforts are also being made to refine such courses by incorporating explicit training in qualities like empathy and compassion that benefit others and society as a whole. These courses offer a comprehensive framework for the cultivation of social, emotional, and ethical skills beginning at kindergarten and continuing through higher education and beyond. I place great hope in a new generation who will grow up with an educational background that includes focus on cultivating the heart as well as shaping the intellect.

Hope for the Future

As we enter the second quarter of the twenty-first century, we find the world is being drawn more closely together by remarkable advances in science and technology. Industry and international trade have produced a global economy, and worldwide communications are eliminating ancient barriers of distance, language, and race. The world has become a global village.

Today, we need to accept the oneness of humanity. In the past, isolated communities could afford to think of each other as fundamentally separate. Nowadays, however, events in one part of the world, whether they concern grave problems of dwindling natural resources or the climate crisis, eventually affect the entire planet. Therefore, we have to treat each major local problem as a global concern from the moment it begins.

We can no longer invoke national, racial, or

ideological barriers without destructive repercussions. In the context of our interdependence, considering the interests of others is clearly the best form of self-interest.

I view this as a source of hope. The urgent need for us to cooperate can only strengthen humanity. It will help us recognize that the most secure foundation for a new world order is not simply broader political and economic alliances but every human being's genuine practice of love and compassion. To secure a better, happier, more civilized, and more stable future, a world in which we all live in peace and harmony, each of us must develop a sincere, warm-hearted feeling of brotherhood and sisterhood.

Whatever the circumstances, we should always look on the bright side. Feeling downhearted can be a source of failure. We must remain confident, patient, and persistent.

Today, the situation in the world gives us cause for concern. If we continue to view the problems we face from a short-term perspective, future generations will face tremendous difficulties. We must recognize that we all want to be happy and none of us wants to feel pain. Therefore, with a clear sense of the oneness of humanity, we must work wholeheartedly for the benefit of our human brothers and sisters. Peace will only be achieved if disputes are settled through dialogue and mutual respect, not through violence and the use of weapons. It saddens me to see so many people suffering as a result of conflict, in Ukraine, in Gaza, and other parts of the world.

I firmly believe that each of us can contribute to making this world a better place now and in the future. I appeal to everyone who shares a concern for lasting world peace to cultivate a sense of universal responsibility and an appreciation that only on the basis of kindheartedness will we lead a meaningful life and make our societies more compassionate and just. Let us be compassionate, not just to our friends and family, but to everyone.

ལྷ་མོ་ཆོས་སྐྱོང་ལ་ན་མོ།། །

Photo Credits

Cover: Kenro Izu

Frontispiece: Richard Gere

vii: Manuel Bauer

xi: Sonam Zoksang

xiii: Raghu Rai

2: Herb Ritts

7: Raghu Rai

17: Jetsun Pema

25: Herb Ritts

30: Richard Gere

35: A. T. Steele

42: Herb Ritts

51: Manuel Bauer

64: Nicky Vreeland

About the Author

His Holiness the Dalai Lama is the spiritual leader of Tibetan Buddhists, a Nobel Peace Prize laureate, and a global advocate for compassion and peace. He promotes harmony among the world's religions and engages in dialogue with leading scientists. Renowned for his erudition, open-minded scholarship, meditative attainments, and humility, His Holiness often says, "I am a simple Buddhist monk."

About Wisdom Publications

Wisdom Publications is the leading publisher of classic and contemporary Buddhist books and practical works on mindfulness. To learn more about us or to explore our other books, please visit our website at wisdom.org or contact us at the address below.

Wisdom Publications
132 Perry Street
New York, NY 10014 USA

We are a 501(c)(3) organization, and donations in support of our mission are tax deductible.

Wisdom Publications is affiliated with the Foundation for the Preservation of the Mahayana Tradition (FPMT).